MILLYS ALTMAN

YEAR OF THE FLU

This book is a work of non-fiction. The names, characters, and incidents are my memory of the 1918 flu pandemic as recounted to me by my parents, Beatrice and Holbert James Nixon.

Copyright 2017 by Millys Altman

All rights reserved

Cover design by Abigail Altman

Formatting by Polgarus Studio

TO THE MEMORY OF MY PARENTS

Chapter One

THE FIRST WARNING

Before he called his first patient for his afternoon office hours, Dr. Holbert J. Nixon opened both double-hung windows in his physician's office to let in as much air as possible. It was a warm humid day, typical for western Pennsylvania in early September, 1918. The three-room bungalow consisted of a waiting room, office, and small examining room. The walls were thin and not much of a shield from the heat. A small fan whirring on his desk kept the air circulating, but it was still hot and heavy.

Nixon was the doctor for the Cleveland-based W.J. Rainey Company at the village of Revere, its' coal and coke works in Fayette County, Pennsylvania. He was fresh out of medical school when he had an offer from Rainey, and he eagerly accepted it. In Revere, he immediately plunged into work since patients were clamoring for him, and right away, he came up against difficulties that he had not anticipated or was prepared for.

The Rainey Company relied on immigrants to work its mines, and there was no shortage of workers. The United

States welcomed millions of immigrants, mostly from Italy and Eastern Europe, in the early 1900's. As soon as ships docked in New York and immigrants cleared Ellis Island, Rainey hired them and transported them to its' operations in Revere and other sites. So, families under Nixon's care did not have Anglo-Saxon names with which he was familiar. Names, such as Gesco, Viegesci, Larkelasi, Lyioesky, Meheliack, Pallapa, and Puskarich he found hard to pronounce and harder to spell. Furthermore, even simple first names were not easy since every family seemed to have a George or Joe or Mike. And that was not the worst of it. This small company town commonly referred to as a "patch" in coal mining country, was a polyglot of languages and not one of them was English.

Most of these immigrants had been in this country long enough to have some comprehension but it was still not enough. They seldom heard English spoken, and when they were together, they conversed in their native tongue. Nixon was perplexed. How could he treat these people if he couldn't talk to them? How could he possibly get to know them?

The first few days Nixon held office hours were beyond awkward. Each time he faced a waiting room of strange faces anxiously waiting to have a look at the new doctor, he was unnerved at the size of the crowd as his eyes swept the room. Only with effort was he able to keep his composure. Every male patient he addressed as "John," and greeted others with a welcoming smile. It was the best he could do. Names would have to wait until he could remember them, and associate them with a face.

When his first patient sat nervously in a chair opposite his desk in his office, he groped for a way to begin the visit and came up with, "You sick?" It turned out to be the opening he used for years because miraculously it worked. Never again did Nixon worry about the barrier of communication. To his astonishment, a torrent of words poured out as if he had lanced a boil! It was a case of mutual understanding and meeting of minds. His patients only needed an opening for them to take matters into their own hands. They were just as anxious to let him know their aches and pains as he was eager to learn them. With gesticulations and dramatized grunts and groans they gave him answers to questions he could not ask and needed to know. Fingers dug into body parts as if to say, "This is where it hurts."

Nixon did not interrupt the pantomimes or speak, but he nodded encouragement and approval to keep the flow of foreign words coming. He listened attentively to the different dialects and was able to get a sense of meaning since some of the expressions had a close resemblance to English. He observed facial expressions, hand gestures, and skin color. For his examination, he took a pulse, lifted eyelids, and used what simple diagnostic tools he had. He laid two fingers together on a belly, tapped on them and listened for sounds that he had been taught to interpret. Years later, when he worked in the hospital, his peers knew him as an excellent diagnostician. His experiences at Revere were his training ground.

On this warm September afternoon, Nixon took off his dark suit coat, pulled on a white smock, and opened his waiting room door to the usual room full of patients. All were familiar. Four straight-backed chairs with tan leather seats were along each wall of the small room and every chair was taken. Women greeted him with broad smiles, showing gaps in their front teeth, and fanned their faces with paper fans to stir the air and try to keep cool. They were dressed in long skirts and sturdy shoes and wore colorful babushkas on their heads. Several men were having a smoke outside while they waited for their turn. Nixon had a list of house calls to make after his office hours, but it looked as though he might be able to finish up and have time to play with Eileen, his blonde, blue-eyed 14-month-old daughter before supper.

His first patient was a teen-ager with a bad case of poison ivy rash. Next was the Kostelnik's four year-old boy with chicken pox. He expected there soon would be more Kostelniks showing up since there were seven or eight kids in the family. As the day wore on, Nixon heard only the usual litany of aches and pains, nothing demanding an extensive examination, nor did he face a challenging diagnosis. He anticipated getting out of the office at an early hour.

His last patient on this hot humid day was Frank Malosky a young miner with heavily muscled biceps in blue denim overalls. Nixon had treated Frank once for a broken arm, so they were well acquainted. The doctor spoke briefly, but he did not try to exchange pleasantries. Frank was Polish, and he had good comprehension, but his verbal English was limited.

In the office, Nixon motioned him to a chair opposite him.

Frank shivered as he sat down. He crossed his arms and hugged his body as if to control his shaking.

Nixon was instantly alert. Frank's face was flushed, which was to be expected in this heat, but it looked like the flush of a fever. A blue color ringed his lips. Headache, chills, fever, aching. September was not a month when Nixon expected to see these symptoms.

"You feel bad?" Nixon asked in easy friendliness. Regardless of the situation or emergency, he always spoke in a calm voice. It quieted excitable patients and gave them hope.

Frank laid a palm across his forehead and closed his eyes.

Speaking was an effort since his breath came in little gasps, so Frank's recital was short. He was sick when he woke up this morning, but he went to the mine anyway. He needed the money. He tried to work, but he was dizzy and his foreman finally told him to go home.

Frank pulled out a handkerchief and it turned bright red when he wiped his nose. A look of fright crossed his face as though he suddenly realized how sick he was.

On examination, Nixon found that his temperature was 103 degrees, his pulse rapid, breathing labored. This was no ordinary case of the grippe. Nixon instinctively knew that he was looking at his first case of the dreaded "Spanish flu" that had been ravaging the country since April. He had expected to see a case long before this. Type A influenza is a specific disease with a distinct set of symptoms and Frank had them. He was desperately ill.

"You have the flu, Frank," Nixon said sternly. "Go home, go to bed and don't get up." He gave him a white paper packet of aspirin and told him when to take it. Nixon did not have a wide array of medicines in his medicine cabinet. He had digitalis, atropine, quinine, codeine, cough medicine and cold pills, tincture of iodine, pills for female distress, a white salve called Saratoga ointment that he doled out in small round tins and thought would heal anything, and other assorted medicines. But he had nothing specific for influenza.

Nixon always tried to give patients a few words of encouragement at the end of their visit, but he could not think of anything to say to Frank. He was too concerned. As contagious as the flu was, Frank might be the first case in Revere, but he would probably not be the last.

Chapter Two

THE VILLAGE OF REVERE

Revere was a reflection of Old Country living. Immigrants brought the ethnic customs and living patterns from their homeland to their new country. It was a congenial friendly community once people settled in and got acquainted. William J. Rainey built Revere around 1900. In the late nineteenth century, mining bituminous coal was a lucrative business. The coal was soft, easily mined, found in pure thick seams, and nationally known as some of the finest high-volatile metallurgical coal in the world. Rainey's first venture was in 1879, and from there he expanded his holdings and became well established in the industry. By 1904, he owned 32,000 coke ovens employing 18,000 men and owned 60 coal towns. Revere was one of them. He was known as the Cleveland Coke King, and he was the most important of Henry Clay Frick's competitors in the Connellsville Coke region.

Revere is the name that everyone uses for this village, but the official post office address is Uledi, Pennsylvania, which is on the other side of the main road in another jurisdiction.

Actually, there were two Reveres. Revere #1 was a mine and coke works, and Revere #2 was a mine only, but both were at the same location.

The village was laid out in a simple grid and was built to be self-contained. Rainey was noted for building more single family dwellings than other mining companies in the region in order to keep a steady work force, and Rainey also had a reputation for building more substantial houses than Henry Clay Frick although most of them were still jerry-built of cheap materials. Identical semi-detached double frame houses were built in rows. They were stiff, bare, cheerless structures painted in ugly red, green, brown or gray, sometimes in alternating colors. It was said that the different colors of the houses were the origin of the word "patch", since the colors resembled the patches in the patchwork quilts that the women sewed, although these were pleasingly colorful.

None of the miners' houses had running water or electricity. There was an artesian well in the center of the village that supplied water, and it was carried in buckets to the houses. Children could often be seen carrying water, and especially on wash day when there was a heavy demand. A school house where classes were held through the eighth grade sat along the main road.

Each patch house had a large back yard, and the residents took advantage of every inch of it. Chicken coops occupied considerable space and supplied fresh eggs. There were pens for pigs, rabbits, and goats, and dogs and cats ran everywhere. On wash day in good weather, yards were full of flapping clothes on clothes lines. Digging coal with a pick and shovel was dirty work, and coal dust permeated everything. Women rubbed clothes on wash boards until their knuckles were raw to try to get the black clothes some semblance of clean. Among other chores, women baked bread in outdoor ovens with thick brick and concrete walls, usually one day a week, eight and ten loaves at a time. Bread was the diet staple.

In the summer, the company store supplied seeds, and large gardens were planted in rows and carefully tended. Competition was keen as to whose garden was the most productive. In the fall, the houses reeked of the strong cooking smells of cabbage and onion, and garlic as the harvest fed them until early October. In July, children roamed the countryside to pick buckets of blackberries for wine making. Canning kept everyone busy in the rush to salvage all of the fresh produce they could before the first frost. Canned goods fed them through the winter.

The company store was a large substantial frame structure where miners were expected to spend their pay. It supplied all of the families' needs from food to furniture that the residents could not make or grow themselves. The quality of the merchandise was good, but Rainey charged top dollar for it. Meat was salted and dry cured and hung on hooks, and canned goods lined the shelves along the walls. Workers paid with a round metal disk about the size of a silver dollar that had the miner's check number stamped on it. A miner's check number was his identification everywhere.

The Rainey miners were paid every fortnight, and they

lived from payday to payday. The average pay was about $35.00 a month, depending on the job, or less than a thousand dollars a year. If a miner went into Uniontown to a saloon on a Saturday night and spent all of his pay, the company would let his wife borrow from his next pay check so the family would not go hungry. Many families were never free of debt to the mining company. Revere did not have a church so priests from neighboring communities came to hear confession, serve communion, and minister to the people. Nixon always resented that the priests demanded money for their services even though the miners could barely put food on the table, but he understood that these priests' visits were as important to the mining families as their daily bread.

A branch line from the Coal Lick Run branch of the Pennsylvania Railroad had a trolley stop in Revere. Residents could board a trolley and ride the three miles into Uniontown or ride to other stops on its route. The trolley provided access to the world beyond, and riding to other destinations was an escape from the hum-drum of life in the patch.

Rainey operated a slope mine on the eastern edge of Revere until the late 1920's. The mine entered the ground at an angle and cars were loaded into and hauled out of the pit along this angle. Double tracks sent down an empty trip and hauled up a loaded one at the same time. The mine floor was uneven. Close to the mine entrance were the buildings and workings that included an engine house, a tipple, trestle, wash and supply house and a stable, among others. Within walking distance was a 60 ft. x 30 ft. club house used for meetings, first aid work, welfare and social activities. It was a gathering spot with a large assembly room, a pool room, and a dining room and kitchen.

Along the north boundary at the height of production there were 650 coke ovens, two rows of rectangular ovens and one bank of beehive ovens, named for their shape. The rectangular ovens at Revere were the second of only two of these types in the original Connellsville Coke Region. Fiery furnaces lit up the night sky, and the soft glow could be seen for miles. It was a mark of the great prosperity of the region.

Chapter Three
ONSLAUGHT

Nixon was shocked when Frank Malosky died within forty-eight hours. Shocked to realize that he was close to death when he was in his office. Frank was young and strong and healthy, and the doctor had fully expected him to recover. By the time of his death, his whole body had turned a dark color from lack of oxygen.

Paradoxically, it was Frank's youth and physical condition that had probably enabled this killer to strike its lethal blow. The influenza virus of 1918 spread through the HINI type. The immune systems of young and healthy adults mounted a massive response to this invader in a cytokine storm, an overreaction of the body's immune system. This response filled the lungs with fluid and other debris and blocked the exchange of oxygen, which was necessary for life. Children and middle-aged or older adults had a weaker response and often did not become as sick.

Death from illness generally strikes the old and infirm and the very young, but the 1918 influenza proved to be an exception. One of the ways that it killed was by quickly and efficiently invading the lungs in an action compared to scorching the lining. It cruelly took its greatest toll on young people in their twenties and thirties, those in the prime of life who should have had a long life expectancy. In the worldwide toll of victims, the most deaths were in this age group, and as many as 8 to 10 percent of young adults then living may have been killed by the virus. Just as the Civil War had affected population growth in its aftermath since men of marriageable age were simply not available to women looking for a mate, so did the flu epidemic affect population growth in the 20's and 30's following the 1918 spike in deaths of young adults in their productive years.

Frank's sudden death brought panic to the patch with loud weeping and wailing. At the end of summer and with no signs of the disease that had been sweeping the country since spring, people had been lulled into thinking that Revere had escaped the epidemic. Remoteness had protected them. But, all through the summer months, the virus was constantly mutating, strengthening and growing in intensity. In infecting human after human, it was adapting to its environment, reproducing more efficiently, and growing in virulence. It was undergoing the phenomenon known as "passage." When it emerged again in August, the second coming was a killing inferno. It began killing at an alarming rate.

Revere was caught in the lethal second wave that traveled to nearly every hamlet, village, outpost and remote corner of the world, even to the Arctic. It lurked on every doorstep ready to rain illness down on anyone who ventured out. Fear gripped everyone's heart and intensified as it took one of their own.

Mothers gathered up their children, paralyzed by the thought that one of them might get sick. They pulled their doors shut, and stayed indoors. To ward off disease, they resorted to Old Country customs. They ate raw onions, put potatoes in their pocket, and hung garlic strings around their own necks and those of their children. They prayed.

The Rainey mine ceased regular operation and remained open with only a skeleton crew. The school house providing classes up to the eighth grade closed. Nixon ceased holding office hours. The usually noisy village became silent with little movement on the dirt roads. Revere folded up like a tent. Who would be next?

The answer came quickly. The incubation period for the flu is three to five days. It is highly contagious, and before a person can feel any symptoms, they may already have affected others. Five members in Frank Malosky's family became sick. His heartbroken girl friend, Anna, was stricken and also, two others in her immediate family. Calls for the doctor increased hourly. Nixon was now certain that he was facing an epidemic of the Spanish flu, and it was deadly. In Revere, people lived in close contact, ripe for the spread of illness. Nixon knew how excitable they were, how easily frightened, how superstitious, how prone to believe old wives' tales. He faced the days ahead with a gut-wrenching fear.

The first order of business was to hire nurses. Nixon realized immediately that he was going to need them. He contacted every nurse that he knew, tried every source that he could think of, and he could not find a single nurse. Even Rainey with all its resources was not able to help him. Other villages were affected, too. In May, 1918, roughly sixteen thousand nurses were serving in the military. The army recruited nurses, and left the civilian population to fend for themselves. Through their "Home Defense Nurses" the Red Cross mobilized women to help, professionals or not. In the cities, the demand for nurses was so great that the few available nurses were accepting bribes to work. The possibility of enticing a nurse to come to a rural outpost of immigrant people was hopeless.

Twenty-eight years old, barely out of medical school, Nixon faced an epidemic that would soon sicken an entire village without any assistance or outside help. It would be a life more complicated than he could ever have imagined when the people of Revere entrusted to his care became ill. Nothing in his medical training had prepared him for what would be the ultimate challenge of a long career. So that fateful September in 1918, the doctor's ordeal began.

Chapter Four

A HUMBLE BEGINNING

Holbert Nixon was born in Olphant Furnace, Pennsylvania, a small hamlet in a valley beyond the last ridge of the Allegheny Mountain. The family soon moved to nearby Fairchance which is not too many miles from Friendship Hill, the home of the first Secretary of the U.S. Treasury, Albert Gallatin. At the time that Gallatin built Friendship Hill in 1789, the land was mostly wilderness, and Nixon's ancestors were already settled in the area, having emigrated earlier in the century. The family prospered. A Nixon tavern served guests alongside the National Road in the early 1800's. From 1828-1841, Nixon's grandfather, Samuel, was an Associate Justice of the Court of Common Pleas of Fayette County. In the early 1900's the population of Fairchance was about a thousand.

From time to time industries flourished there. Early on, iron furnaces produced a high grade of pig iron that was made into cannon balls and shipped down the Mississippi River to New Orleans. The cannon balls were used by General Andrew Jackson in the battle of New Orleans. Coal mining was the main industry for many years, but the mines shut down at the end of World War II.

Nixon was named for the doctor who delivered him, Dr. James Holbert. Nixon was short, about five feet five inches tall, with a broad face, dark brown eyes, and dark wavy hair. His medical year book picture shows him with his hair combed in a pompadour on one side of the part. Possibly with youthful vanity, he thought it made him look taller. He was thin with a slight build like his father, Samuel, but otherwise he looked like his mother, Harriet. She always called him Holbert, but everyone else called him "Nick." A daughter was the oldest in the family. Nick was the second child and first son in a family of seven children. His brother, Bill, was next in line and three girls followed. It was a fortunate gender sequence for good family relationships, two boys and then three girls followed by one last boy. Edgar was the youngest in the family, and Nixon was sixteen years old when he was born. As might be expected, Ed always looked to his brother as a father figure.

Nixon's father, Samuel, was superintendent of the United Brick Company whose red bricks lined many of the streets in Fairchance. With his work in the brick yard, Samuel did his best to support his large family. They had plenty of milk and eggs since he kept two cows and Harriet tended to chickens, but money was scarce. Christmas presents were few, and one of Nixon's memories of the day was the gift of an apple or an orange when he went to the Presbyterian Sunday school.

As a child, Nixon's mother would make him wear one of

his sisters' dresses when he misbehaved. Quaint though this discipline was, (and psychologists would undoubtedly frown on it today), it was part of an upbringing that instilled the qualities of duty, hard work, devotion and kindness in the children of the family.

Fairchance did not have a high school until 1915, so, Nixon and other students had to travel on a West Penn trolley 7.2 miles from Fairchance to Uniontown to further their education after elementary school. The orange trolley passed in front of Nixon's house every half hour which made boarding easy. Nixon was a good student, but he had to drop out of school when his father lost his left eye in an accident at the brick yard. Suddenly there were hospital expenses and a family to feed with no income. Nixon was forced to go to work while his father recuperated.

Then, as if that weren't enough hard luck, a severe mountain storm took the roof off the family home. Fairchance sits in a bowl and the winds coming from the west and southwest hit the side of the Allegheny Mountain as they pass through the bowl and come rolling back down, picking up speed and causing destruction. Nixon had to work until the roof could be repaired and prolonged the time before he could go back to high school. His classmates were long gone when he was finally able to attend classes again, and he was twenty years old when he graduated.

With the help and encouragement of his namesake, Dr. James Holbert, he was able to go to Jefferson Medical College in Philadelphia. He graduated in 1914 and his oddly phrased year book description says, "He goes to his roost early, but gets up earlier and acquires his stuff." Nixon came back to Uniontown to serve his internship at the local hospital, which had opened on Thanksgiving Day, 1903. It was a frame building with three gabled roof sections and a screened porch on one side. It stood on a large grassy plot on the west end of town. The doctors were all local, and through his time with them, Nixon developed life-long friendships.

Motorized vehicles were in common use, but the ambulance that transported sick and injured patients to the hospital was horse-drawn and looked like a big box on wheels. It ghoulishly resembled a casket. It was not equipped with bandages or splints or medical equipment. Critically ill patients, most of them men injured in the coal mines, endured a bumpy rough trip. One ward of the hospital, subsidized by the mining companies, was devoted to these patients. Fractures and head injuries from falling slate were frequent and required the most care. The rest of the hospital was rarely full. It did not have a maternity ward since most babies were born at home in the care of a midwife.

During the first year of his internship, Nixon met the nurse who was to become his wife. Beatrice Berner was born in Freeland, Pennsylvania, in anthracite coal country of eastern Pennsylvania and graduated from high school in Hazleton. She was a graduate of the Protestant-Episcopal Hospital in Philadelphia. Nixon was in medical school at the same time she was in training there, but they only got to know each other when she moved west to be the night superintendent at the Uniontown Hospital. Bea grew up in coal country, and she felt at home in the western part of the state since the landscape was not much different from what she was familiar with. But travel was difficult and distance kept her apart from her family after her marriage.

Bea was the same age and as tall as her husband. She had thick curly black hair and cheeks that always had a rosy color. The position of night superintendent did not have the status that the name implies today. Besides nursing patients, Bea did hard necessary work to keep the hospital running smoothly. In the early morning, she would fire up the coal stove in the kitchen so that it would be hot enough to cook oatmeal for the patients' breakfast when the cook came in. One morning when she was tending the stove, a sudden flash of fire burnt off much of her beautiful hair, but fortunately it did not burn her face.

At the end of his internship, Nixon married Bea in Hazleton and they honeymooned in Atlantic City. Several months after their return, Nixon was pleased to accept an offer from the W. J. Rainey Company to be the physician for the Revere mine. Treating families in a coal patch was not exactly a dream job, and he wanted to be in private practice, but he did not have enough money saved to pay expenses for the time it would take him to get established. He also felt that he needed experience before he struck out on his own. Nixon was a general practitioner, and so were most doctors in 1918. Specialization in medicine was years away.

Nixon signed an agreement to care for the four hundred residents in Revere for a dollar a month for each family (extra for obstetrical cases). That meant care for all family illnesses and most of the families were large and increased in size almost yearly. When the mine siren sounded that there had been an accident, Nixon had to drop everything and rush to the mine. He could send serious injuries to the hospital in Uniontown, a three-mile trip, but he was expected to treat everything else. The contract provided him with a steady income for the first time in his life, and a home, rent free. It was just as well that he did not know of the experience that awaited him. His offer didn't turn out to be much of a bargain in 1918.

Fortunately, Bea Nixon came from hard scrabble coal country or she might have been dismayed at the bleak and unattractive home in Revere that she came to as a bride. The house with a lone pine tree in the front yard faced the main dirt road and was at the western end of a row of mine officials' residences. These houses were larger and more securely built than the other patch houses, even so, they were not built with design or aesthetics in mind, and all of them were the same. Each house was two and a half stories with three bedrooms, a bath upstairs, an ample kitchen and dining room downstairs. In the winter, coal furnaces kept the houses warm in the day time and also layered the rooms with black dust that came through the open registers. At night the coal furnace was banked, and if Nixon had to go out on a call, the house was cold. Next to Nixon's home was his office bungalow, last in the line of buildings. Down his back steps, across a short walk and Nixon was at his office. He moved to Revere with all the enthusiasm of a young doctor thrilled to have his first practice. He and his wife happily settled into the simple pleasures of life in this little village.

Then, suddenly, Nixon faced the threat that he might have to leave Bea and his baby daughter and his established life in Revere. On 6 April, 1917, the United States declared war and joined the conflict that was being fought in Europe. The first draft call was for males between the ages of twenty-one and thirty and Nixon fell into this age group. Later, the draft call was increased from ages eighteen to forty five, but subsequent draft calls were cancelled when army camps became overwhelmed with influenza. The army was aggressively recruiting physicians and the real possibility that Nixon would be drafted overshadowed everything. It was an anxious time. On June 5, Nixon registered with the local draft board in Uniontown. Fortunately, he did not have to wait long before he received a Class 4 classification, which meant that he was deferred. As a doctor, his services were deemed essential. Revere needed a doctor. Nixon's younger brother Bill, however, was not as fortunate. He was single, a bank teller in nearby Fairchance, a nonessential occupation, and he was notified that he was classified for active duty.

Chapter Five

A VILLAGE IN CRISIS

In ordinary times, after his office hours, Nixon would crank up his Model T Ford and set out in the patch to go down his list of house calls. He would be greeted with waves and smiles as he traveled from house to house carrying his heavy black satchel. Now, with the flu invasion, regardless of the hour, the dirt roads were largely deserted and hardly anyone was to be seen. People ventured out to get food from the company store and water from the well, got necessities as quickly as they could, and disappeared. Essentials at the company store soon became in short supply since the transportation system was disrupted and the store wasn't getting deliveries.

If Nixon stopped at one house, word spread that he was there, and the minute he stepped outside, he was beseeched with pleas from frenzied family members for him to stop at their house next. His mere presence was in itself a source of comfort since people believed in the omnipotence of their doctor. Nixon carried the heavy burden of their faith and trust, and he was deeply affected by it. People knew that this was flu, but it seemed to have no relationship to past attacks when they could expect misery for eight to ten days and that would be the end of it. This flu was entirely different. It attacked its victims suddenly, and some would collapse without warning.

Symptoms were alarming and followed a common pattern: extreme fatigue; headaches so intense people thought their head was going to split open; aching joints; severe nosebleeds; and in the later stages, bleeding from almost every orifice in the body; painful earaches; gasping for breath and forceful coughing. The disease attacked the respiratory system and penetrated deeply into the lungs. Lungs that were normally soft and spongy became firm and solid and could not transfer oxygen into the blood stream. Patients' lips would turn blue and, as the illness progressed, their bodies would gradually become a ghastly dark color.

Nixon could not answer every summons and cry for help. He had to close his ears to the pleas and set his own course. The days were not long enough for him to see every patient. He visited the sickest patients first, where he knew the need was greatest. Doors were never locked, so he did not hesitate to open a door and walk in after a knock. He did not expect to be greeted. This Catholic community could not show its usual charity to take care of others. Those who might have helped were either frightened, sick, or too busy taking care of their own. The communal spirit where everyone pitched in and helped when illness or misfortune struck vanished.

Bedfast families were too ill to open their eyes, let alone answer his knock. Nixon found patient after patient cyanosed, gasping for breath, so sick that when they rolled over, they crackled from pressure on the pockets of air just below the surface of their skin leaking through their lungs. When he found patients in this condition, he did all that he could to try to keep them alive. There would be no one else to help them. He was the only person many of these families saw for days.

Of necessity, Nixon became both doctor and nurse. He checked vital signs, brought water to the bedsides and replenished the aspirin supply, all the while speaking cheerfully. He emptied slop jars sitting by the side of the bed, although some were too weak to use them or to clean themselves. Some patients had pre-existing conditions exacerbated by their sudden illness that had to be treated. Nixon could not take the time to clean the soiled beds, but he did his best to leave his suffering patients more comfortable and in better shape than he found them.

When Nixon entered the bedroom of the Karpiak four-room house, two little sisters, five and seven, were huddled together under a worn patchwork quilt. They were blue even under their fingernails, and both of them were unconscious. He often saw the two blonde girls with their high cheekbones and blue eyes, so common to these people of Slavic descent, as they hopped and skipped to the artesian well in the center of the patch and filled buckets of water to bring to their mother.

As he approached the bed the mother, Anna, spoke briefly to him in a whisper. He looked into her troubled red-rimmed eyes and felt a quick rush of sympathy. He wished from the depths of his weary body that it was within his power to heal her little girls, but he could not save them. Anna knelt beside her husband before a statue of the Virgin Mary in a corner of the room to pray. The parents knew the little girls were beyond temporal help, and they had turned to Almighty God. As they prayed before the flickering light of a single candle on the altar, Nixon stood motionless at the foot of the bed. Tears pressed against his eyes and he turned away. What the parents needed was a priest who spoke their language to say what they wanted to hear, to comfort them and pray. He was not that person so he quietly left the room.

According to historian John M. Barry. "Influenza is a viral disease. When it kills it usually does so in one of two ways: either quickly and directly with a violent viral pneumonia so damaging that it has been compared to burning the lungs; or more slowly and indirectly by stripping the body of defenses, allowing bacteria to invade the lungs and cause a more common and slower-killing bacterial pneumonia."

In the midst of the epidemic, two children in the Kostelnik's family came down with the chicken pox as well as three in a family living next door. Since Nixon had already diagnosed one Kostelnik child, the mothers knew what they were dealing with, so he let the advice he had previously given suffice. Fortunately, none of the children took the flu, even though several family members were sick. Nor did any suffer complications. A chicken pox epidemic did not materialize, and Nixon attributed it to the fact that the school had closed and children were kept indoors.

Nixon did not have oxygen to give patients who gasped for every breath, and even if he had, oxygen had proved to be of temporary value where it had been tried. Nor did he have access to the new techniques that surgeons developed during the epidemic to treat infected lungs. The air at Revere was contaminated from the effluvium from the coke ovens and was not healthy to breath at best. Nixon found Albert Kozlowski's father pitiful in his agony of afflicted coughing lying in a suffocating room with one small window. With heroic determination, Nixon devised a way to get air into the room and into the man's lungs. He rounded up men to knock out one wall of the house. The miners were well-muscled, but it took several sweaty hours of pounding, ripping and pulling before splintered wood from the house siding was a pile on the ground. The old man was more comfortable in the warm September weather, but the drastic effort did not save him. He lingered for another two days and died of bronchial pneumonia struggling for breath while a blood-tinged froth gushed from his mouth and nose.

The demand on Nixon's time was so great that most days he hardly had time to come home to grab something to eat, or to change into fresh clothes. At the end of a visit with the Puskarich family, he was counting out pills on the hard kitchen table when he suddenly pitched forward, face down, in a deep exhausted sleep. He slept in this cramped position as two adult members of the family tiptoed around him until he finally jerked awake. He sat up, and without a word continued to count out pills as though nothing had happened.

Rose and Joseph Agostini were from different provinces in Italy, but they met on the boat coming over and married soon after they came to the patch. Rose was nineteen, full of energy, always cooking and baking and giving handouts to the neighbors. And then she came down with the flu. Two days passed, and when she wasn't getting better, Joe became alarmed and called the doctor.

"Rose, you'll feel worse if you don't do what I tell you," Nixon said. "Stay in bed and don't get up. Let Joe do the cooking."

The next day was Sunday, and devout Catholic that Rose was, she couldn't face Sunday with a dirty house. She took a dose of the doctor's pills and got up. Joe protested, but on her hands and knees, she scrubbed all of the floors in the house. The next afternoon, Joe came for the doctor. Nixon knew immediately that Rose hadn't listened to him. He expected to find her desperately ill, and he doubted that there would be much that he could do for her. With a heavy heart he answered the call, but he was unprepared for the scene that awaited him in the Agostini bedroom.

Rose was lying on her back with her hands folded holding a crucifix. Her eyes were closed. She was dressed in a white wedding gown with a billowy veil bunched around her thin shoulders. Artificial orange blossoms circled her dark hair. For her last day on earth, Joe had fittingly dressed his bride to meet her Maker.

Nixon was tormented that he had only aspirin to offer to relieve the extreme suffering. Penicillin and antibiotics were years away for treatment. In October, the Surgeon General of the United States Army and the Journal of the American Medical Association both recommended very large doses of 8.0-31.2 g. of aspirin per day, and Nixon followed the guidelines. Aspirin helped to relieve the severe body aching. But to him it seemed to be a betrayal of his medical training that he had to face an illness and combat it with this as the only remedy. He could not turn to his medical books since the "Spanish flu" was unknown when he was in medical school.

In normal times whenever he was presented with baffling symptoms, Nixon would find a reason to ask the patient to come back. In the late evening hours at home, he would turn to his medical books. Nixon relied heavily on his instinct and the information in these books. He would read until he found an answer to his immediate problem and could make a diagnosis. He did not have the option of ordering tests since few diagnostic and blood tests were yet available, and even if they had been, his patients could not have afforded the extra expense.

One day in the thick of things, Nixon happened to meet an older doctor of his acquaintance on the main road traveling in the opposite direction. Both stopped their Model T's, to talk about what was uppermost in their minds. Nixon was quick to inquire what this gray-haired doctor's treatment was, hoping to draw on his experience. He wished profoundly to hear remedies other than what he had, and that he felt must be out there. The doctor said, "I've found rest is the best thing. Give them aspirin. Tell them stay in bed." His own advice! His disappointment was acute.

Instead of coming away with information he could use, this chance meeting only added to his frustration. He felt as though he was fighting a battle without weapons or ammunition.

Nixon was not alone in his frustration. Scientists felt as helpless as he did in the face of this killing monster. Laboratories worked feverishly to find the pathogen that caused the flu, trying experiments and new techniques, anything that showed promise, working against the pressure of time. People were dying by the thousands, and no one, not even the best and the brightest minds, could come up with an answer that would stop the killing.

Chapter Six

WHO WOULD BELIEVE?

As a complication of the flu, every pregnant woman contracting the disease had a miscarriage or delivered a premature baby. When the first premature baby was born alive, Nixon faced a dilemma. What to do with this baby that would need special care? The mother was in danger of losing her own life, too sick to care for a robust newborn let alone a fragile one. Nixon did the only thing he could think of. He wrapped the tiny infant in a thin blanket, laid it in a wicker basket on the leather seat of his car and brought it over the bumpy road home to his wife.

Bea was a resourceful, strong-willed woman, and she loved a challenge. When Nixon walked into the kitchen with the baby in his arms, she was vigorously rolling out dough on the kitchen table. She looked up, surprised to see him.

"Mary Favrek's. It's a boy," he said.

Bea shook her head in dismay. Mary was young, no more than eighteen, and this was her first baby.

"Do you think you could?" Nixon left the question hanging and searched her face.

Bea wiped the flour on her hands on her apron, and reached out to take the bundle. She held it close. Lifting the corner of the blanket, she gazed at the sleeping baby's tiny wrinkled face, and nodded that he was now hers to keep alive.

In due time, one by one Nixon brought her seven mewling babies to care for in addition to her own 14-month-old daughter, and she welcomed each one as if it were her own. She was determined to save every one of them.

Bea turned an upstairs bedroom into a nursery. The Rainey Company was anxious to do anything to help, and when word got out that Bea was caring for the preemies, the company store sent over supplies: Arbuckle wooden coffee crates, sheets, bottles, diapers, blankets and other necessities. Bea lined the crates with pillows and hot water bottles, and the babies slept snug and warm. She and her 20-year old hired girl, Mary, cared for them. Mary was a strong girl, a Slovak, who lived with them full time, and seldom took time off to go home. She was next to the oldest of ten brothers and sisters. To keep the babies alive was a constant vigil. Bea and Mary took turns sleeping at night, and neither of them got much sleep.

During this time, Bea and "Nick", as she called him, saw very little of each other. She always prepared supper, and he made an effort to get home so that he would have at least one good meal, and they would have some time together, but more often than not, he didn't make it. Bea would set his food aside and warm it for him when he showed up. When he was there he checked on the preemies and gave Bea advice.

Some babies required more care than others. The weakest

baby was the daughter of the mine foreman who lived next door. Bea and the baby's mother were good friends as well as neighbors and exchanged gossip, recipes, and homemade dishes over their shared backyard fence. Bea desperately wanted to save this premature baby whose shallow breathing was barely keeping her alive. She fit into Bea's outstretched hand. She and Mary kept a constant watch over her because without any warning, the baby girl would turn blue when her tiny heart faltered. When this happened, Bea would pick her up, rush into the bathroom and lower her into a sink of warm water. With an eye dropper, she would put a few drops of brandy in her mouth. Then, she would gently massage and massage the fragile body until her circulation improved and her color returned. It was a constant battle, not only with her, but sometimes with several of the other babies, and it seemed to be fought most often in the lonesome early morning hours.

Also, as if she didn't already have her hands full, through the worst of the epidemic, Bea cooked huge pots of vegetable soup and oyster stew every day. The company store kept her supplied with ingredients. Nixon told her where help was needed, and she gave out house numbers to healthy teenagers to deliver the soup to the weak and the sick. With a gauze mask protecting their faces, the teenagers fanned out over the village carrying hot soup, drinking water from the well and kindling wood for stoves. They would give a sharp knock on the back door of each house and, without waiting for the door to open or venturing any further, they would place the supplies within reach and leave. For many families, the soup kept them from going hungry until they could cook something for themselves.

Bea cared for each baby until Nixon thought it was strong enough to be given back to its mother and the mother was recovered enough to have it. However, she couldn't just hand over a baby. The mother had to be taught to care for it, and Bea took on this job, too. There was no one else to do it. Her greatest happiness came the day she handed her neighbor her baby daughter, and a grateful mother held her firstborn, small and skinny, but crying lustily, pink and alive. And she was not the only grateful one. Miraculously, Bea saved every one of the seven babies.

Chapter Seven

THE RAMPANT VIRUS

The source of the 1918 flu pandemic will always remain a mystery, although there are several theories. Perhaps the most accepted is that it began in late March in Haskell County, Kansas, where a severe influenza was raging. From there visitors brought it to Camp Funston, an army base that was the second largest cantonment in the United States. From Camp Funston, the disease rapidly spread to other camps. As it spread insidiously through the troops, so it began to spread among the civilian population. This first spring wave caused thousands to be sick, as it raged throughout the world. Thirty of the largest cities in the United States, most of them adjacent to military facilities, experienced an outbreak. The flu swept through neighborhoods, killing indiscriminately. Every family was at risk. Terrified people locked their doors from the invader but were stricken anyway. Cities were at the mercy of the virus. Men feverishly dug graves to bury the dead as bodies piled up, and sometimes forklifts dug a trench and filled it with bodies.

In May, two months after the outbreak, Bill Nixon was called for active duty. His family hardly had time to accept the fact that he had to go when he was gone. Bill and several of his buddies boarded a street car in Fairchance, and were transported to Fort Lee, Virginia for training. With the best of intentions, in a burst of empathy, Bea sent him a chocolate cake to Fort Lee. "Thank Bea for the cake," Bill said in one of his letters, "but I will never get it." In six weeks, he was in Hampton Roads, Virginia aboard the S.S. Madawaska, (formerly the Koenig William II) bound for France. By the summer of 1918, America was sending 10,000 fresh troops to France every day.

American troops brought influenza with them. Cases appeared in France in April and struck with alarming force among troops stationed at Brest, France, when the Camp Funston divisions arrived in early May. Brest was a deep water port, and it was the port of entry of almost half of the American troops in Europe. Thousands of men in close contact were sickened and put out of action, but nearly all of those troops recovered.

Other European countries suffered outbreaks during the summer. Ships coming into port brought the disease with them. It touched Africa and reached Bombay by the end of May when a transport harboring the disease docked, and from there it spread to other cities in India. It reached Shanghai about the same time and swept through China. New Zealand was affected, and it reached even its remote villages. Australia imposed a rigid quarantine on incoming ships so its death rate was low even though the disease finally penetrated the country in late 1918. A few places escaped and one of them was American Samoa. Not a single person there died of influenza since the governor imposed a quarantine, and a blockade of ships coming into port. In the United States, the East and South were hit the hardest. The flu reached California and the West with fewer cases, and the Midwest was the least affected. Native American villages suffered heavily.

Spain was neutral during the war, and newspapers were free to print the news without fear of censorship. Reports of influenza, the seriousness of the disease and deaths were published. Not so in censored French, German, and British newspapers where nothing negative was printed that might hurt morale. Stories of the Spanish outbreak were picked up and published in other countries, and thus the disease became known as the "Spanish influenza."

However, although flu slowed the German offensive and thousands were affected, it did not strike with much force. In fact, British doctors questioned that it was actually influenza. The infection was mild and caused pain in muscles and joints, fever, severe headache and general misery. Most influenza patients recovered fully in 10 days. By late August in Britain, the flu had largely disappeared, and it was publicly declared that the epidemic was over.

The virus, however, had not retreated. All through the summer months, it was constantly mutating, strengthening and growing in intensity. In infecting human after human, it was adapting to its environment, reproducing more efficiently, and growing in virulence with the "passage."

When it emerged again in August, the second coming was a killing inferno. It began killing at an alarming rate.

The second wave was so lethal and widespread that it affected the outcome of the military action in Europe. Initially, the German offensive was proceeding well, and the advancing army seemed unstoppable, but neither side was able to deliver a decisive blow for two years, in 1915-1917. Then, Germany launched Operation Marne (Second Battle of the Marne). An allied counter offensive known as the Hundred Days Offensive began in August 1918 with a decisive German defeat. It was known as the "black day of the German army." German commander Erich von Ludendorff blamed influenza as one justification for his defeat. His fighting forces were weakened by disease, and reports of illness were widespread.

The second wave reached an extreme of virulence unknown before in any other widespread influenza outbreak in history. It killed more people in a year (about 50 million) than the war itself killed (about 16 million, military and civilian) in four years. It is estimated that more people were killed in this epidemic in a year than the Black Death in Europe (1347-51) in a century.

As prevalent and serious as the flu was in America, by August in France, when Bill Nixon's unit arrived at St. Nazaire on the Loire River, it apparently was not seriously rampant, at least in this area. In the official report of the 319th Infantry, American Expeditionary Forces, there is no mention that the flu affected any of the men. Nor did Bill mention flu or illness in his letters, although it is possible that the news was censored.

The unit travelled by train in a forty-eight hour ride across the country to Calais with thirty to thirty-five men and their equipment crowded into each small light rail car. If anyone had had the flu it would have spread rapidly with men crowded together.

Bill wrote that France "was so far behind the times that it will take a thousand years for them to become civilized like the people in the States." One thing he noticed was that the natives in St. Nazaire wore wooden shoes. Tired and thirsty men could not drink water randomly since water had to be treated, and there was not an abundant supply of fresh water. "You don't have to strip at night and dress in the morning," Bill wrote. "You just sleep in all the clothes you can find." That meant sleeping on the hard ground. Living conditions were deplorable and certainly ripe for the spread of illness, but Bill did not get sick.

Chapter Eight
SEARCH FOR A CURE

By some miracle, Nixon, his wife and little daughter did not become ill although they were exposed to the flu every day. He took no precautions, accepting the risk as doctors do without thinking about it. What would happen to his patients if he got sick never entered his mind because he expected to take care of them. He pushed himself to the limit of his endurance, and exhaustion should have made him easy prey for illness, but neither he nor Bea became sick. It was a blessing, and Nixon had no reason for it. They were both born in 1890, so the immunity could not be attributed to illness acquired in the flu epidemic of 1889-90. It defied explanation.

New cases of the flu kept cropping up every day, and with no seeming end to the epidemic. Some disgruntled suffering people lashed out at Nixon and accused him of having some magic preventive medicine that he kept for himself and was holding out on them. The accusation was both preposterous and unfair, but Nixon knew that no argument would convince these desperate people that he was playing fair with them. He simply had to live with the criticism and not let it bother him.

Revere was not alone with people clamoring for medicine to combat this illness. The influenza virus was unknown to scientists in 1918. From the time of Hippocrates until the nineteenth century, for a span of more than two thousand years, medicine had remained virtually unchanged. Doctors did not probe beyond their observations and reasoning. When medicine began to use objective measurements and mathematics combined with the use of microscopes and scientific experiments, the practice of medicine began to change. Germany became a leader in the scientific community. European medical schools were subsidized by the state and could afford to give students rigorous scientific training while American schools without outside support did not have that luxury. America lagged woefully far behind, and scientists from the United States often traveled to Europe to study.

By the Civil War, America began to advance, however slowly. As late as 1900, many U.S. medical schools would accept any man-but not woman-who paid tuition. Standards were very low at most medical schools, and only one required a college degree for admission. A high school diploma sufficed for most.

Then, in 1873, John Hopkins died and left a trust to found a university and a hospital. The university opened its doors first and, not until twenty years later, in 1893, did the Johns Hopkins Medical School open. It was a huge success. By the time of the flu epidemic of 1918, with brilliant work done by the Hopkins in Baltimore, the Rockefeller Institute for Medical Research in New York, and some universities, America had caught up with Europe. A handful of American leaders emerged and worked to transform the life sciences and medicine.

Among scientists, there was a huge race to find the pathogen that caused influenza. Cries for help from the public put enormous pressure on them. Laboratories worked feverishly to develop a vaccine. The pressure was so great that several laboratories offered vaccines to the public only on the wishful hope that they would work. There was not time for trials to prove their efficacy, so there was no guarantee. A government agency like the Food and Drug Administration to step in and exert some control was years in the future. In fact, despite the urgency, it would be more than ten years later, in 1928, that the influenza virus would be identified in papers published by Richard Shope.

Since doctors did not have any approved scientific treatment, in desperation, many tried their own cures in an attempt to save lives. Results didn't bear them out, and some of these bordered on the absurd. The percentage of deaths from these random experiments was high, but, even so, many claimed success. A few even resorted to the long discredited remedy of bleeding. The Journal of the American Medical Association published therapies that doctors tried, anything that seemed to make sense, without endorsing any of them.

Cautious by nature, Nixon did not experiment, nor was he temped to try any of the suggested therapies. But he did take one drastic step on his own. He quit dispensing aspirin to relieve the awful aching. Rose Agostini's death taught him a lesson. He learned from his own experience. Nixon knew that the disease had to run its course, and if you got up from your sick bed too soon, it would come back to bite you. He observed that the patients who listened to him and stayed in bed, survived, and the ones who refused and kept on going developed complications or died. Men would feel better and plunge into work after a week or two and then collapse and die without warning. There was a thin line between life and death. Body aches were so intense that people could hardly move. Yet, to force patients to take his advice and stay in bed, he decided to withhold aspirin and deny them temporary relief as a life-saving measure.

The scientific explanation for sudden deaths came years later. With their immune systems compromised, secondary bacterial infections invaded the patients' lungs and they died from pneumonia. It is generally agreed among scientists and epidemiologists that the majority of influenza deaths in the pandemic came from bacterial pneumonias.

Late in the epidemic, a vaccine became available named after Camp Sherman, a military camp in Ohio whose morbidity rate had been the highest in the country. Nixon was fortunate to be able to obtain a supply of the Sherman vaccine, as it was called, so that he could inoculate people, although he didn't hold out much hope for it. As he expected, the vaccine proved to be ineffective and was just a panacea. Although it didn't help his patients, it benefited him immensely. People in the patch were reassured and felt protected, and the unwarranted criticism he was getting stopped.

In late September, Nixon received word that his brother, Bill, a corporal in the 319th infantry, had been killed in France on September 26, 1918. On that day, the Meuse-Argonne offensive was launched by the French and American troops for a final assault on the Hindenburg line. This was the largest United States offensive of a war that had raged for four years. Bill was killed by a direct hit from a shell, and his death came just a little over a month before the armistice, November 11, 1918. He lost his life in this last big battle of the war, just four months after he left the States, and three days before his 25th birthday.

This news of Bill's death was a crushing blow. It came when Nixon was exhausted, engulfed each day in sickness and overwhelmed with the sorrow of others. Close in age, he and Bill had shared a happy childhood. Nixon wanted to go home. He wanted to be with his grieving parents, not only for their sake but for his own. He needed the comfort of family. But he had to put aside his personal grief. He could not leave Revere in distress without another doctor to take his place.

Chapter Nine

LIFE MOVES ON

The flu epidemic that invaded Revere without warning, caused untold anxiety, and wrecked havoc with the health of the inhabitants suddenly disappeared in about six weeks, vanishing like a fading light. Natural processes began to work just when it seemed as though the influenza virus would bring about an end to the human race. The virus had mutated from a mild form in the spring of 1918 to a deadly killer in the fall. When it reached this extreme, any new mutations were more likely to make it less lethal, a mathematical concept called "reversion to the mean." And this is exactly what happened. It began to lose maximum efficiency and, also, the population developed as least some immunity to it. Once the virus could not infect unimpeded, new cases dropped off precipitously. In 1919, a third wave of influenza came, but it was less virulent and Revere was not affected.

While the epidemic lasted, it took a terrible toll. In Revere, every household was affected. There were nine deaths. At its peak, Nixon singlehandedly cared for almost a hundred seriously ill patients. Those who developed the flu toward the end of the epidemic had a milder case. Compared to other towns, the death rate was low, but the figures don't tell the story of the depth of the emotional cost. This was a close-knit community. Families had come to America together. In the patch, everyone knew everybody else, and each death was personal.

As infectious as influenza is, after a bout with it, someone may have lingering symptoms, coughing and sneezing, but usually in no more than a week they will not infect anyone. People recovered slowly and ventured out timidly with disrupted and broken lives and never to be forgotten memories. For many there was never complete recovery. Permanent kidney damage and damage to other organs was common, weakness lingered. The Revere mine resumed normal operation. Children returned to school. The steady hum of activity in the patch slowly increased. Life returned to a new normal. To show their love and affection for their devoted doctor, women showered him with freshly dressed chickens, fresh eggs and bread and home baked pies. Raisin pie was his favorite.

Influenza is an endemic disease, it is always around, and it has caused deaths for centuries when a new virus emerges. Scientists have developed effective vaccines against this killer, but there is no cure yet available. New pandemics are almost inevitable, and no one can predict when this will happen.

One afternoon, soon after Nixon resumed regular afternoon and evening office hours, a woman from an outlying farm about a mile from Revere appeared. He was surprised to see her by herself. He saw her infrequently, and she was always with her husband.

"You got troubles, Mary?" the doctor asked kindly as he looked at her weary lined face.

"It's Joe," she said. She nervously twisted a handkerchief between red and swollen fingers. "Him in bed. Six weeks I milk the cows, slop the hogs, feed him."

"What's wrong with Joe?"

"Lazy good-for-nothing. You say, Joe, you have the flu. You could die. Go home. Go to bed and don't get up until I tell you to."

Nixon heard the echo of the mantra that he had spoken a hundred times. In the thick of things, thoughts of Joe were blocked out when he had -seriously ill patients crying for attention.

"Oh, Mary, I'm sorry. I'll come today, and give you a rest."

He held her arm and gently led her to the door. Then, he sat down in his swivel chair, and with his head thrown back, he laughed a deep laugh that rolled out in waves as he released the tension of weeks.

About the Author

Millys Altman was born March 16, 1921 in Uledi, Pennsylvania, (Revere) the village that is the setting for this book. The family moved to nearby Uniontown, Pennsylvania, when she was four years old. She still lives there.

She graduated from Hood College with a degree in Home Economics, which she taught in a local junior high school for two years. In 1942, she became a war bride, and for the next three years she followed her Navy Lieutenant husband to wherever he was stationed. When his beach battalion unit embarked for the Pacific, she came home.

After the war, Altman's husband practiced architecture, and she had a family of three sons. She didn't start to write until the boys were in their teens because she never could find the time. Besides nurturing the boys, she was a companion to her husband who was a great outdoorsman. He taught her to hunt and fish, and they traveled all over the country for sporting trips. For three weeks every fall, they floated the Snake River and hunted deer and antelope in Wyoming.

Altman's husband was a car buff, and like father, like son, so were the boys. The older two became professional sports car racers. Altman bravely went to the tracks and watched them race their Porsche, and out of her experiences came her young-adult novel *Racing in Her Blood*. For her next book, she turned the many enchanting stories of her small town that she heard growing up during the golden age of the coal and coke era into an historical mystery *Innocent Strangers*.

Altman has enjoyed life under sixteen presidents, and still swims and plays bridge.

Visit Millys at her website www.millysaltman.com

Email Millys: maltman@atlanticbb.net

Innocent Strangers—https://amzn.com/B008J1XIK6

Facebook: http://facebook.com/millys.altman/

Made in the USA
San Bernardino, CA
02 May 2020